GOD *for* GROWN UPS

God *for* Grown Ups

NEW ways to think about the BIG questions

Bob Garrity

Aware Village Press

Aware Village Press
20 Sunnyside Ave. #121
Mill Valley, CA 94941

www.AwareVillagePress.com

press@awarevillage.com

Library of Congress Control Number: 2011905432

ISBN-13: 978-0615472058
ISBN-10: 0615472052

Printed in the United State of America

Dedication

To my many teachers, family and friends who have helped me along my path and filled my life with love. Especially to Oscar Ichazo, Iqbal Lewis, my Arica Men's Group (David Downey, Alan Woontner, Mark Johnson, Dieter Gloeckler, Gary Karp, Bob Lucas) Larry Steutzel, Jessica Jones and the Arica School; my Saginaw buddies (Dean Baumann, Pat Shawl, Dave Waddell, Jim Picard, John Hanley, John Wells, Mike Hanley), my dear friends Robin Retallick and Eva Gregory, my Mom and Dad; my brother – Bill, my sister and niece – Leslie and Kelsey; and my darling wife (and editor) April, the love of my life.

CONTENTS

The Big Questions

We all have life defining moments – marriage, the birth of a child, getting that dream job, etc. For me a life defining moment came in August 1972 on the top of a mountain in Colorado when I was 19 years old and on a camping trip with some friends. It was a beautiful day and I was right on the continental divide with mountains stretching in every direction.

I decided this was a good place to do a little meditation. At that time I was a beginner, I had just started meditating a few months earlier and I was not a regular practitioner. As I sat down and began to meditate I had my usual results – a mind full of chatter, I was not able to quiet it all. And then I was blessed with an amazing experience.

I went into a deep state and my mind became very quiet – I was totally present and aware of all around me and yet I felt almost outside my body. And then I moved into an even deeper state and I felt an overwhelming joy and it felt like the universe had opened up.

It was all clear to me – that we live in an amazing creation and that everything in the universe is absolutely connected to everything else. All of this was to me clearly vibrational, it seemed like everything was patterns and waves of energy connecting all. It also felt clear that there was an overriding intelligence to it all.

This amazing state lasted probably a total of five minutes, and yet it was so profound I can still feel it clearly 40 years later and I will talk about the experience more later in the book.

Since that powerful event I have been on a journey to understand those deeper questions many of us ponder – Does God exist? If so what is the nature of God? What is my true spiritual nature, my connection to God? And the big one – Why am I here? After 40 years of study, meditation and spiritual pursuit I believe I have some of the answers.

The title of the book is *God for Grown Ups*, and the central idea is that a concept of God as a father figure, or some being "out there", is comfortable to children but it doesn't really answer our questions of the nature of reality, and it doesn't really show us what our true reality is.

This book contains my thoughts, understanding, and beliefs on these questions. My hope is that this book can be of interest and help to people who are looking for answers to those questions posed above, those who feel those questions have not been answered by their current religious teachings, and those who see themselves as agnostic and perhaps even atheistic.

A belief in God or some form of a higher power is almost universal. A Baylor University study done in 2005 found that 92% of Americans said they believed in God or some form of a higher power.

The percentages are as high or even higher in most of the rest of the world, the exception being Western Europe. But even in France, which has the lowest percentage of believers of all European countries, according to a 2005 Eurobarometer report, 61% of the population believes in God or a higher power.

The Baylor University study also looked at what people thought was the basic nature of God or this higher power and how much they felt God engaged in human affairs. The study was then able to break these belief systems into four basic types:

Authoritarian – This group sees God as judging everyone, makes rules that must be followed, God can be angry at those who do not follow his rules and can be very involved in the world's affairs. This is a view of God that demands strict adherence to the rules and punishment of those rules are broken. 31% of people fell into this category.

Benevolent – This group believes God sets rules on how we should live but is forgiving of anyone who repents their sins. God can intervene in human affairs on occasion. Overall God is seen as loving and can be described as a Father figure. 23% fall into this group.

Critical – God does set rules and is judgmental but does not interfere at all in human affairs; judgment happens after you die. 16% believe in this way.

Distant – This group sees God as a cosmic force and not as a being. They tend to believe that God created the world but then allows it to be left to its own. Some believe we can tie into the energy of God. 24% of the people fall into this category.

But what if all of the above ideas about God were wrong in some ways? What if the way we were taught, as children, to think of God had some fundamental flaws and no one ever taught us anything differently as we grew up?

If the way we think about God were to change dramatically how would that affect our lives in a personal manner and in the way we interact with each other? How does organized religion, despite good intentions, actually get in the way of people getting in touch with their true nature?

Those subjects, and the big questions posed earlier in the chapter, are the ideas that will be tackled in this book. The goal is to come to an understanding that how we look at and imagine God, our fundamental ideas of the nature of God, needs to become more expanded and more mature and in doing so we will be opening ourselves to immense power and the possibility of immense change as individuals and for humanity as a whole.

Beyond the Finite

As can be seen from the previously referenced studies, a huge majority of people do believe in God (for the rest of the book we will use God for any belief in higher powers as well). This makes the question of how people view God extremely important. Someone's basic understanding and belief in the nature of God will affect how they view the world and how they may view their fellow human beings.

I had an encounter with this question on the nature of God many years ago when I was a student at the University of Michigan. I took a philosophy class which was a general overview of Western philosophy, and the assignment the teacher picked for our class term was to prove or disprove the existence of God.

When she first announced the topic I was thrilled. This was after my Colorado mountain top experience and it was a question to which I had already devoted many hours of reading, some time in meditation, and long discussions with friends.

However, my excitement soon turned to disappointment when the teacher, who was actually a graduate student only a couple of years older than me, laid out her ground rules for the question we were to tackle. She said that we had to define God as an omnipotent, all-knowing, all-powerful being who could and would interact directly with us, a being that could change anything at any time and affect individual outcomes. In other words, she insisted on a definition of a God that could come down from the mountain, so to speak, and judge you, save you or even kill you, namely the God of the Old Testament.

She cut off any other definition of God by saying that if we were defining God as just a force in the universe or as an energy beyond our physical understanding, but God did not interact with people directly in the way she outlined, then that God was irrelevant.

In her view, if there was no direct interaction of God into our lives as a physical presence then that was not a meaningful question to worry about. She basically said only the first two types of God outlined previously (Authoritarian and Benevolent) were relevant and dismissed any other type of belief in God.

This was a big problem for me; she was defining God in a way that I knew was not real and in a way that I knew would make it easy to disprove the existence of God. We had quite a debate about her parameters and her refusal to accept other definitions of God, as I was not the only one in class that held other views. For me it was a matter of principle and I would not give in and spent the whole semester arguing my points, bringing in ideas from Buddhist and other Eastern philosophies and trying to get her to agree that there was another way to look at God – in fact what I thought was the right way to look at God.

Of course she did "prove" that God did not exist – given her narrow definition. However, even though I never gave in to her point of view I still managed a C in the class, one of the proudest C's I ever had.

Her view of God, as an authority and/or father figure is a quite common view of the nature of God. However, I have come to understand that this view of God actually is a limited view. This is not meant in any way to insult anyone, but total honesty is needed in this area.

The purpose of this book is not to disparage people's beliefs, their religions and what they think about God, but it will be an attempt to get people to look at the nature of God in a different way. We need to let go of the way many of us were raised and to see that this view of God as an omnipotent judge or father figure is, as we said before, a limited or narrow view. God is much more than that.

This view of God as a father figure, as a judge, as the figure with a beard on the ceiling of the Sistine Chapel does not stand up to scrutiny. As I saw with my philosophy teacher, it is not hard to prove this God does not exist.

Where does this being live? Why would an omnipotent God set up rules knowing that humans would not follow them? Why would a loving God show mercy sometimes and not at other times? Why would God reveal himself to some but not to others? One would come to the conclusion that God is sadistic and/or capricious.

But, again going back to the above studies, many people who see the flaws in the idea of God as a "man in the sky" still do feel there is some form of a higher power. They then often draw the conclusion that God is simply a cosmic energy, perhaps resembling "the Force" from Star Wars.

Some others feel that God created the universe but then is removed from it. Or they take a more agnostic view that God is beyond our knowing so we should just focus on our lives here. This is the "distant God" from the previous categories and people in this group often do not see God as being important in a personal sense.

The truth – as I have come to understand it – is that while it is a mistake to think of God as some sort of judge or father figure, this truth does not diminish the idea or importance of a personal relationship to God in any way. When we begin to recognize the true nature of God we see it is a most profound and important aspect in all our lives.

God is not something "out there" but something inside of us, a part of us. And this truth that God is with us all of the time means it is impossible not to have a personal relationship with God. The questions then become – what is the nature of that relationship and how aware are we of the relationship?

It is natural to think of God as a being – as something having a personality. This is the way we relate to all other people we encounter. We see others as distinct beings that we interact with. Even inanimate objects are conceived of as things with distinct boundaries – we know their general shape and substance. We know that something with four legs and a top is called a table, even though we may see a table design we never saw before we instantly know it is a table.

Our minds like to put things in the proper "box". And in fact we have to do that to make sense of our surroundings. So when contemplating God, and certainly as children trying to understand God, it is only natural that our mind will conceive of God the same way it conceives of any person or thing we come in contact with – we want to put God in a "box".

But the problem in defining God in this way is that when we create a concept, or "box", in our mind for people and things these "boxes" are part of our physical world of time and space. God is not part of that existence. God is beyond time and space. When we conceive of God we must always remember that we are trying to *define the infinite with finite terms* and there is a limit to that. Lao Tzu, the founder of the Taoist tradition, said it best – "The Tao (Infinite Way) which can be spoken is not the true Tao."

Trying to put God in a finite "box" will never give us the correct view. We have to let go of all preconceptions and look beyond normal experience to understand the true nature of God. That is why all the great spiritual teachers have had transcendental experiences in their lives that were the keys to them waking up to the true nature of God and of their own divine nature. And that is why ultimately the knowledge of the Divine is something that on some level has to be experienced to be understood fully. However, we can get a taste of it through study and meditation so for the purpose of this book we will continue on a quest to understand the Divine as best we can with words.

The question then arises – if God is beyond our physical world of time and space, is there anything that we experience and can relate to that could be seen as being beyond physical limitations? There is only one thing that we experience that can be freed from strict ties to time and space – consciousness.

Many philosophers, spiritual teachers, and even modern scientists have come to the conclusion that the energy which makes us aware of ourselves goes beyond just the physical aspects of our brain and body.

Certainly we understand that they are linked – when our body ceases to function our consciousness in this physical plane also ceases. It is beyond the scope of this book to engage in the huge discussion of consciousness, the brain and metaphysics. But there really is no full scientific explanation for all aspects of the nature of consciousness and I know that is in part because consciousness goes beyond our time-space reality.

What if it is true that consciousness is in fact part of the eternal non-physical reality that is beyond time and space? What if your consciousness existed before you were born and will continue to exist after you die? Now we can begin to understand the concepts of a soul, a divine spirit and its connection to God. When we study all of the deep teachings of all the great religions and spiritual Masters we see they are all teaching that we are, in fact, eternal beings.

If we accept this then we can see that the energy of consciousness is the thread that ties us to the eternal. When we decide to manifest into a physical life this eternal consciousness actually divides itself – part of it becomes attached to our physical selves and begins to evolve into our ego-personality self.

The other part of consciousness remains connected to the divine energy of our eternal self. It is known in different traditions as the Soul, Divine Consciousness, the Higher Self or in Eastern philosophy the Atman.

As we grow and develop from birth – the ego consciousness, because it is dealing with the physical time-space reality of our daily lives, becomes dominant and the eternal divine part of our consciousness fades into the background.

This eternal consciousness is in fact a direct emanation of God and since we are still connected to it, God is with us at all times. As our ego-personality grows stronger we lose that connection and, in fact, all spiritual teachings are ultimately simply a journey to remember and awaken that Divine Self. As we reawaken to the energy of this Divine Consciousness we can in a very real sense be connected to God – the God that is within us and within every human being.

We thus see that our consciousness is energy, and that an aspect of that consciousness is divine energy. God is in fact better understood as similar to the energy of consciousness, much greater than we can imagine of course, but God is not some physical entity or some personality.

When it is said that "we are made in God's image" this is what is meant – God does not have a body – God is pure energy, the same as the energy of consciousness. We see that through the energy of consciousness we are incarnations of divine energy. We are *divine beings having a human experience* and that is a really, really important point to understand for yourself and for the world and for humanity to move forward.

As we are going to see in the rest of this book, this concept of God changes the game. When you no longer have a God that is laying down rules and regulations on how people need to live and punishing you if you don't live a certain way, then it changes the world and it opens the world up.

And when you recognize that all humans have a Divine Consciousness within them it changes your interactions with your fellow Divine beings. And finally we can best describe the nature of this divine energy as pure love.

In the rest of the book we will explore further these three fundamental truths:

1. *God is within every individual equally – we are all One with God.*
2. *God does NOT make rules and free will is the dominant force in creation.*
3. *The fundamental nature of God and of our Divine Self is love and compassion*

My Early Years

Who am I to be talking about all of this? I am definitely not a guru or an enlightened master – I have had the privilege of being taught by enlightened masters and I definitely have not attained those levels of accomplishment.

But I have spent almost 40 years in pursuit of spiritual knowledge and have been blessed with some experiences of pure divine transcendence which have had a profound impact in my life. Through these experiences and teachings I have come to a deep understanding of some aspects of consciousness and the Divine which I wish to share with others.

My early spiritual training was, like many Americans, in church on Sundays. My father was raised Catholic and my mother was raised Methodist and when they got married they compromised on Episcopalian, which is kind of Catholic "lite." It was funny because my father agreed to that compromise and then never went to church. He basically gave up on church at that point other than going maybe at Easter and Christmas.

So, it fell to my mom to take us to church. We went fairly regularly but not every Sunday. We moved a couple of times so I was late doing catechism and getting confirmed. I think for most kids that happened when they were maybe ten or eleven years old.

I was twelve or thirteen by the time I received that confirmation ceremony and to do that I did have to study the bible some, but it never really caught on with me, it just did not sing to my soul. So at 15 I decided I did not want to go to church anymore and my Mom agreed that I was old enough to make that decision.

So, that was it for a while. I didn't really do anything spiritual. But the one thing that was always a spiritual constant for me was being out in nature. I often went camping and hiking and spent summers in Northern Michigan as a swim instructor and camp counselor at Scout camp for two summers, and one summer at YMCA camp.

In addition to being out in nature, I also got some life lessons. During those summers I often hung out with guys who were already in college and we had a lot of spirited talks, not to mention the fact that I learned a lot of nasty language and how to play poker.

Some of those talks did revolve around God and the nature of everything. For me this ultimate question really came down to something fairly simple, which is that this universe that we are in is either a creation or an accident. It is either something that has a conscious creation behind it or it is something that just came together out of basically random coincidences.

Now some would argue that the universe and nature began to order itself and that then order was created out of chaos, but there was no original force or intelligence behind the resulting order.

However, that is really just a variation on the random chance argument since it would be just as likely that no order was created – without any guiding principle behind it the fact that the universe was able to order itself would still be just dumb luck. If order was inevitable then there was something else going on that made that order inevitable.

If in fact the entire creation including life itself is an accident, if the formation of galaxies upon galaxies and universes upon universes is just an accident, and if the formation of life itself is just a random event of some cells that came together and created life and then evolved all the way up to human beings, then that is it.

In that case you don't really need to look any further. There is no need for any spiritual seeking; we live in a random universe. We live and then we die – end of story.

That would also mean that human consciousness is nothing more than an effect of our brains which have also evolved over time, because there would be no reason or sense for consciousness to exist apart from the physical aspect of the brain.

On the other hand if it does not seem like life and all of existence is simply accidental, what are the implications of that conclusion? Is there any proof to support that position? It is beyond the scope of this book to cover all the areas in science that have shown us the incredible connections and synchronicities that exist in our world and our universe. But we can see some very clear cases that support this idea.

For example – we know the conditions necessary for life to form are so amazingly narrow that for life to have actually happened seems to be more than just a random coincidence. We know that scientists have not been able to recreate any conditions that allow a group of chemicals to jump the gap into being alive – so how did that happen?

We also see patterns in nature repeated over and over. Connections in the way stars and galaxies are formed and evolve repeat themselves over and over. And some of these patterns occur all the way from the macro level of stars and galaxies down to the micro level of atoms.

Even more than that it seems obvious to me that our consciousness is greater than just what could be explained by mental activity. As stated before, no one has a clear picture on consciousness and the brain, but there are certainly many examples, such as out of body experiences, where consciousness seems to go beyond the limits of the physical.

Then if you come to the conclusion – as I have – that this is a creation, then there has to be a creator, some energy and intelligence that made the creation. So, to me, the ultimate proof of God's existence is simply that everything points to the fact that we live in a creation which means there must be a Creator.

If you come down on that side of the argument – that we live in a wonderful creation and that everything is working together in some way – then you have to believe in God, whatever way you want that to be. Then the question becomes the one we are exploring – what is the nature of that God that has created all?

So as a teenager I was leaning toward a belief in God but was still questioning and had no real spiritual practice or understanding. I then went off to school at the University of Michigan in Ann Arbor. And it was during this period of my life when I awakened to my true spiritual nature.

My Awakening

In college I was exposed to different ways of thinking and one set of ideas that caught my attention right away was Native American spirituality, because I had always loved the outdoors and their spirituality revolves around nature.

As I said, I was a boy scout and I'd been camping all my life. I spent summers as a camp counselor in northern Michigan and so a nature oriented spirituality really appealed to me. Reading about Native American beliefs definitely was something that spoke to me and opened up a different way of thinking about spirituality, which saw all of creation as part of God and God was in every aspect of it. That instantly made sense to me.

Then in the spring of 1972 I joined many of my generation and tried hallucinogens. I took LSD and that had a profound effect. Obviously drugs are still a controversial topic in our society, but we are now at a point where researchers are objectively studying the effects of hallucinogens on people and finding that they can have life changing, positive effects – which was certainly the case with me.

Doing acid broke down all the barriers of consciousness and opened me up to a new way of thinking, a new way of seeing. My ego dissolved for a while and I felt truly one with the cosmos, as they say, and it changed my perceptions in the ways that Aldous Huxley wrote about in *The Doors Of Perception*.

Once you realize that your perceptions are part of your thinking mind, and that when your perceptions change it will change your interpretation of reality, that is a profound realization. It forces you to look at all of your assumptions about reality.

This questioning led me to start exploring different philosophies and that led me to Zen Buddhism. I first read *The Way of Zen* by Alan Watts and then *An Introduction to Zen Buddhism* by D. T. Suzuki, who at that time, was the most authoritative Zen teacher writing books for Americans.

The philosophy behind Zen Buddhism also really resonated with me. I immediately felt a connection to what they were talking about in terms of the ego state and our consciousness and how the ego state needs to be quieted.

Zen appears to some as a nihilistic philosophy because it deals with the negation of the ego, in a sense taming it, and how the ego thinks of itself as supreme and the need for one to get beyond that. But in fact Zen is not nihilistic because once the ego is tamed, so to speak, there is an underlying sense of peace and even joy. This all rang true to me from what I had already experienced.

I started to practice Zen meditation, basically from reading about it and going to one or two classes. There was a Zen center in Ann Arbor but I did not attend any classes regularly. While I did like what I was reading about I have to admit I was never into the robes and at that time not disciplined enough for the aspects of a heavy meditation practice.

I really did not have much success with the meditations. As any beginning Zen practitioner will tell you, it is hard to learn to clear your mind, which is the heart of Zen practice. For most people it takes years and years of practice to be able to get to the deeper meditative states.

This all took place in the spring and early summer of 1972 when I was nineteen. Then in the late summer of that year I had that profound experience which still influences me to this day. Three friends and I took a camping trip to the Rocky Mountains in Colorado.

What happened to me was that I got a little bit of altitude sickness when we got there, so I didn't feel very good, I didn't feel like eating, I didn't want to drink any beer or smoke any pot and I just ended up for a couple of days fasting unintentionally and drinking water out of this clear mountain stream that was right next to our campsite. We were camped at an altitude of about nine thousand feet. So I did this unintentional fast and cleansing and then by the third day of camping I was feeling better so I ate a little food and we took a hike.

As I said, we were camped about nine thousand feet and we hiked up this trail maybe another fifteen hundred feet and ended up right on the top of the continental divide in Colorado. It was amazing and a gorgeous day, the mountains stretching as far as the eye could see and the sky was clear and bright blue.

We ended up perched on the slope of a mountain top with a crystal blue little mountain lake right below us, and we were right above the tree line but there were trees right below us. I sat down and thought to myself "this looks like a nice spot to try to meditate."

I sat down and started to breathe deeply and slowly and to watch my thoughts float by to try to bring myself into the meditative state. Every time I had done this before I had, at most, felt a little peaceful, but my mind never quieted down very much. This time it was different, very different. My mind really quieted down, after a few minutes it seemed like I had no thoughts, just a quiet peaceful feeling. After a few more minutes of this I suddenly went into a deep, deep state of awareness.

My eyes were closed but I became totally aware of a rock off to my left. I'm sure I'd seen it before I sat down, but I just had this sense of the rock being there and exactly what it looked like and that I was totally connected to it. And then there was a cricket chirping off to my right and I just felt like I could see that cricket clearly even though my eyes were closed.

Then all of a sudden the wind whistled in my ear and my consciousness was set free. It felt like the top of my head had come off with a feeling of pure energy and I saw a sort of green yellow light in the center of my head.

At that moment I knew, with all my being, that everything and all objects and all people in the world were just patterns of energy and they all interacted with each other. It was immediately clear that everything was connected to everything else and that it was all composed of energy, everything was part of this amazing field of light and energy and it was crystal clear that we were also all part of it. It felt like the whole universe was filled with wondrous light.

I had no sense of a self, no sense of "me" – just a sense of connection to all. I also had a clear sense that this all had an amazing intelligence to it, it was no accident. It was a deep experience of a larger reality, this complete, total awareness that we are one with all of creation and that God is in everything and that we are part of God.

I would say the whole experience from going into a deeper state to the "top of my head coming off" probably did not last more than a few minutes, maybe even less than that. And then I had this thought of, oh my this is great and of course that "me" thought immediately brought me right out of that state because that transcendental state is a non thinking state. If you have any normal type of thought then you are not in a transcendental state.

This was the moment of my real awakening. I never have forgotten the experience; it has influenced my entire life from that point forward. I can still close my eyes, almost forty years later, and be right there on that mountain. It was that powerful an experience.

Afterwards I was thinking, wow that was great, now I know how to meditate! Imagine my disappointment the next day when I sat down in my tent at the camp ground to meditate and my head was just filled with chatter, chatter, chatter like it had been every other time.

I thought – oh what happened, where is my beautiful meditative state? I felt irritated and confused and I did not meditate the rest of the trip. We returned to Michigan and I went back to school in Ann Arbor where I did try to meditate a little bit but had no more success at quieting my mind than I had before the trip, and at that point I was really frustrated by it.

It just so happened that about a month, maybe six weeks after this event – right at the beginning of that school year – Roshi Philip Kapleau, one of the first Zen Roshi in America (Roshi is a Zen term for priest,) came to lecture in Ann Arbor and I went to see him.

He gave a lecture which I enjoyed immensely and at the end of his talk people were asking him questions. Someone asked a question about satori, which can be understood as a Japanese term for enlightenment, or an enlightened state would probably be more accurate. This person asked him if reaching satori is the end goal and he said, "Oh no, no, no. That is just the beginning!"

He said that you can reach satori while you're dancing, you can reach satori watching a sunset. You can have moments of this enlightened state at any point in time in many different ways and that is not the end – that is the beginning. It is when you've tasted that state that you realize – okay this is where I want to go.

Hearing that was a great relief to me, and what I had experienced on the mountain top now made complete sense. I had been blessed with a taste of enlightenment and I have since come to understand that my taste was a little bit deeper than most. But it was really just the beginning of my journey into the Self.

After hearing Roshi Kapleau I understood that satori, even a deep experience of it, was still a beginning step to learning how to have deeper state of awareness on a more regular basis. For whatever reason, I was blessed to have gone to the deepest transcendental state of awareness on that mountain top but that was just the beginning of my path.

Since then I have been blessed to have had two more experiences of going into that deep state of pure awareness. In addition, I have had many experiences of states that were close to that state of pure awareness. And through meditation I have been able to be more in touch with my Divine Self.

Even though I got a lot out of reading about Zen and hearing the Roshi's lecture, Zen Buddhism didn't really appeal to me in the long term. It is a pretty austere practice and lifestyle and at that age I was too much of a party animal to go down that road.

For the next few years what I ended up doing was a lot of reading. I started reading everything about Buddhism, not only Zen Buddhism but Tibetan Buddhism and I started reading some books on Sufism as well. I was also still reading books on Native American spirituality and other books like *"The Autobiography of a Yogi"*.

During this period I moved from Michigan to California, I was living my life and reading and I was pretty much just an intellectual about spirituality, not doing any practice. It was eight years after my mountain top experience when I had the next big jump on my path.

On the Path

In 1980 I was living in San Francisco and working as manager of a small air freight delivery company. As part of my job I made regular pickups at different companies. I became friends with Larry, one of the guys working in the mail room of an advertising company in San Francisco, when I saw he had a number of books on Buddhism and Sufism at his workstation.

I would see one of his books and think "oh wow, I haven't read that one yet". We got to talking about different things and started hanging out together, getting stoned and having long talks on philosophy. Larry was involved in a mystical school called Arica and so we started having discussions about that.

At that time I was very much into the idea that it was better not to be involved in an organized group. It seemed to me at the time that all organized groups inherently break down the true spiritual essence which is individual and free and that if you got in a group mind then there will be rules and regulations and order that would stifle the natural spirituality that we all have. Also from the end of the 1970's to the early 1980's there were a lot of active cults such as Moonies, People's Temple, est, Rajneesh, etc. that made groups seem at the time, dangerous.

Because I had this very anti-group attitude it made me resistant to Arica but we kept talking about it and talking about it and I had to admit I was intrigued. Most of what Larry was saying really made sense to me and I also recognized that I did not have any kind of spiritual practice and I felt that I probably needed one somewhere along the line to develop further.

I had an intuition about needing some sort of practice but still had a lot of resistance. For a few months we kept having long talks and arguments about Arica and different meditation trainings.

Finally one night we were sitting in his apartment and we were both stoned. I was still arguing with him about my beliefs about the inherent problems of any kind of organized group. He just slammed his hand down on the table and said a bit angrily – "if you spent one tenth the energy on trying this stuff that you spend arguing against it, you might find it has some great results!"

I was taken aback but I had to agree with him. I was spending a lot of time arguing about whether or not I should participate in a group rather than just trying it and seeing what the experience was like.

It so happened that there was an Arica event taking place that next month called "Three Days to Kensho", which interested me because Kensho was also from the Japanese Zen tradition – Kensho is similar to satori but more like the first taste of enlightenment, the term for the first awakening when you really get that there is a spiritual aspect to your life and first recognize the dual nature of consciousness.

Larry's outburst convinced me to try this training and he actually got me a scholarship so it did not cost me anything because even thought I was working at that time, I did not have a lot of extra cash laying around.

We went off and did this three-day Kensho training in Santa Cruz and the first night, Friday night, I sat at the back of the room because, even though I liked Larry a lot, I was not yet totally convinced this was not some sort of a cult. I also thought I might just not like it. There I was sitting at the back of the room because I am a pretty big guy and if they were going to try to lock me in they were going to have a problem on their hands.

So I was at the back of the room and I was kind of keeping my guard up, but I was participating. The Kensho training was really an overview of the Arica School at that time. It was a series of video tape lectures from Oscar Ichazo, the teacher and the founder of the Arica School, with some various meditative exercises in between the lectures. As soon as I started listening to Oscar's lectures I was blown away.

Here was someone who was saying exactly what I knew the truth to be. It really fit exactly with everything that I had experienced and had been reading about and it was really quite remarkable for me. Then we did the meditative exercises which I also found to be very powerful. On top of all that the people were very friendly and nobody was locking the doors.

I relaxed and got into it Friday night and by Saturday I was really into it. The lectures were again, just blowing me away. I could not believe that I was hearing something that seemed so correct to me, so right on about our spiritual natures, and especially the way that Oscar Ichazo related it to our times. It was a modern explanation of the mystical truth, the metaphysical truth that I had experienced and had been reading about.

By the end of Saturday I was really enthusiastic about what was going on and I leaned there was a big Arica training coming up that summer. That training was called the forty-day training and is not offered anymore.

It was a six-week, residential training in Hawaii, and by the end of Saturday I was thinking "this is really great stuff; I'm definitely going to keep doing this work. I know I can't make it to Hawaii this year but I'll definitely try to get there next year". This was in March 1981 and the training started in June of that year.

Then we continued the training on Sunday, the final day, and I was doing this work and I was listening to these lectures and doing the exercises and meditations and I really felt like my soul was singing. Even though I had no idea how I was going to be able to do it, by the end of the training on Sunday I vowed to myself and to others around me that I was going to go to Hawaii that year; I was going to make it to the forty-day training.

For the next three months I worked hard and I scrimped and saved. I had to quit my job and I sold almost everything I owned to get the money for the tuition. I was also able to get a reduction on the training fees by doing a work/study scholarship.

As I said earlier, I was working for an air freight delivery company, and because of that I had racked up huge mileage on my car. It was no longer worth the blue book value and it was not worth what I owed to the bank, I just had to give the car back to the bank.

Thus I quit my job, sold everything I owned and ruined my credit to get to Hawaii to do this training – I put it all on the line. But there I was in beautiful Hawaii in June of 1981. And the training was remarkable and it changed my life and along with the mountain top experience it was the single most profound spiritual experience I have had and set me firmly on the path that I have been on ever since.

It was also in Hawaii that I was able to reconnect to my mountain top experience. At the very end of the forty-day, we performed a meditative ceremony called a zhikr. Zhikr comes from the Sufi tradition and is a combination of music, movement and song. It is a very beautiful, fun and powerful spiritual practice.

At the very end of the Arica Zhikr, which lasts about 40 to 50 minutes, all the participants are seated in a circle and singing. As the singing came to an end, and the live music stopped, I took a slow deep breath and immediately went into that transcendental state again. I experienced that green yellow light in my forehead again and the total feeling of pure transcendental oneness. Of course, once again, as soon as I thought "I am back there" – it was gone; but it left a wonderful feeling and I knew I was on the right path.

Since then I continued to do Arica trainings for the next 25 years. I even served on the Board of Directors for the Arica Institute. I have also been involved with a Sufi order. I studied with a Sufi teacher for a couple of years and was initiated into the Chisti Sufi order. I have also taken refuge (initiation) in the Kagyu Tibetan order and I have taken a few Tibetan Buddhist seminars and classes.

But Arica was my main meditation practice for 25 years. I also want to make clear that this book is not in any way connected to the Arica School or the teachings of Oscar Ichazo – these are my thoughts and understanding alone and do not represent any other teachings.

Of course during this entire period I continued to read and study a variety of traditions and modern writers and even modern physics, which is intersecting more with these types of mystical practices.

Then in the last few years I drifted away from Arica some and, through some very good friends, I have been involved with Law of Attraction teachings and it has been very interesting and illuminating to get their perspective on all of these questions about the nature of God, reality and consciousness.

All of these experiences have established in me a firm foundation in the nature of God. Earlier, I outlined what, to me, seem logical reasons for believing in God. There is also the way of "gnosis" or direct knowledge of God. If you have this direct experience of a non-physical reality, then it becomes very clear to you that the non-physical reality is just as real as or even more real than the one that we are in now.

It also becomes obvious that this energy of expanded consciousness that you are experiencing is beyond your physical limitations. When you tap into that energy that is all around us as I did on the mountain top, and as I have been able to do a couple of other times since, you know for a fact that there is much more than the physical reality going on and if that is true, then it becomes clear to you that once your physical existence is over, that non-physical reality is going to keep on going.

Just as we saw that God cannot be seen as finite, the same is true of consciousness. Our consciousness is a focus of energy. It is divine non-material energy focusing in a material plane but also maintaining a connection to the non-physical reality which is eternal, and that is one key to understanding your true nature. To understand that you have a Divine Self that is eternal is very important and we are going to cover that in much more detail very soon.

One of the things that is a bit difficult in explaining this is that I have been blessed to have had these experiences of the transcendental where I have left my physical self and really merged into my Divine Self, and what is a bit frustrating is that it is very difficult to explain that state because that experience is beyond words.

As I said, the minute that you think about that experience, the minute that you go, 'oh this is a wonderful experience' – the experience is over. It is literally beyond thought and words and in fact if you have any thoughts and words you cannot be in that experience. As I mentioned before, in Taoism the famous saying is "the Tao which can be spoken is not the true Tao." That simply means a transcendental experience cannot be put into words because by its very nature it is beyond words.

This makes being on the spiritual path and wanting to help people understand it, to teach them about their divine nature, a somewhat frustrating experience, because you are trying to get people to understand, and even lead them to, an experience that is beyond words when the only way you initially have to do that is with words.

All of these experiences have brought me to where I am today. I think I have something to share about all of these questions on the nature of God, the nature of ourselves, our consciousness, our minds and how all of that relates to God.

I am certain in the existence of God, I know that God is within each of us, I know that there is more to reality than our physical human selves, that there is something transcendental to this material plane. And I know that the real game of life, our purpose in being here, is consciousness.

None of the truths I am talking about are new but I am hopeful the way I deliver the message may resonate with some and be of help in their awakening to their true Divine Self.

The Eternal Creation

I established in the first chapter the central idea that we should not see God as an authority figure or a father figure, or a mother figure for that matter. God is not a person; God is not even an entity because God is beyond any boundaries, beyond any words. God is the totality of everything that exists, and more.

God is eternal and infinite, the Creator, and at the same time the creation. That is important – that God is the creation and we are part of that creation and therefore we are part of God. When I say that we are part of God we have to understand that is not just a euphemism, that is a direct reality of understanding the divine nature of our consciousness and I am going to talk about this in greater detail.

For now it is important to understand that our consciousness as a human being is divided into two aspects. One aspect is the divine energy which is directly connected to God and the other is our human nature which is our ego self, our thoughts, our personality. And it is through our connection to the divine, eternal consciousness that we are, in fact, always connected to God.

Because God is beyond our finite world, all the great spiritual teachings have relied heavily on analogy, metaphors and story telling. By doing this they are trying to get people to think in different ways. To get them to understand this truth that is beyond words.

Analogies and stories allow for ways in which a person's mind might get to a point of understanding that is new and different, that does not follow their already established thought patterns; ways which can break their conventional way of thinking. I am going to create an analogy to try to better understand our relationship to God and the nature of God.

Imagine an ocean, infinitely large, that is filled with the energy of creation, the energy of God. From this ocean, huge rivers of creation flow – each river representing an entire Universe. From these rivers, smaller rivers of creation flow representing galaxies and from these galaxies flow even smaller rivers of suns and planets.

Now imagine a stream of creation flows from one of these smaller rivers and it represents all of humanity – everyone who has ever lived or will ever live. From that stream of humanity a smaller stream flows which is your existence through many lifetimes. From that stream there is a tiny stream of creation that comes out and that tiny stream is the individual consciousness that you are experiencing now.

In this map you are part of the ocean of God even though you are also an individual stream with your own distinct, unique personality. And that tiny stream that is you in this life is tied to a larger stream of you which is more personalities that you have had over different life times and different incarnations and experiences.

And that all flows back to the even larger stream which is our common experience as humanity, as all human beings, and that flows back to the ocean of God which is all of creation, which is infinite, eternal, full of light, love and compassion, and blessed and joyful.

When we understand that the nature of God is this amazing energy of eternal creation then we can recognize that we are actually involved in the whole of creation because we too are a part of this energy of God.

Then we see that all that is going on around us is actually part of our creation, because in a real sense, nothing exists except our thoughts. Our reality is our thoughts and as we create our thoughts, consciously or unconsciously, that becomes our reality. We live in this creation at the same time that we are creating it. We will explore this in more detail shortly.

Now, one thing about this creation is that it is all flowing, it is all connected and because there is no entity up there directing things as it goes along and no one is making rules or regulations, there is also no entity that is going to step in and save you or perform miracles for you. If you perform a miracle it is because you created it yourself.

There are certainly miraculous healings and all sorts of similar things going on, but that is always because it is your consciousness that plugs in to this Divine Consciousness that brings this tremendous energy and it can accomplish many amazing things but also has limitations. The most obvious one being that we are all going to die.

I think this analogy helps us see our connection to God and to the entire creation. It also answers the question of why are we here. We are a part of the energy of God and we are experiencing God's creation and creating it at the same time. We are part of the creation but we are also part of the Creator. We are God experiencing itself.

We also see our direct connection to all of humanity, because we are part of that larger stream as well. This is a very important point because in this way we see we are all truly brothers and sisters. And of course all of the streams are always connected to God. Let us explore that connection some more.

Our Divine Connection

One summer in the early 1980's I attended a week-long Sufi retreat in Mendocino County in Northern California. The Sufi work is very heart-oriented, which means it works to open your heart and increase your feelings of love. The goal of the Sufi practice is to see God as the Beloved One. The famous love poems of Rumi, a Sufi saint, are actually love poems to God. This Sufi group I was involved with worked a lot with music and they were also the group that had started Sufi dancing workshops in the early 1970's.

Toward the end of the week I was walking in the woods in the late afternoon. My heart was very full from all the wonderful meditations and singing and dancing we had been doing. It was late afternoon and the sun was streaming through the redwoods, it was gorgeous, and I thought it looked like a natural chapel.

I stopped and took a few deep breaths to center myself and I felt like my heart expanded even more and all of the sudden everything around me was vibrating and the light seemed almost magical. I actually got tears in my eyes and I whispered – "Thank you God for all of this magnificence."

We see that in this idea of the nature of God that we are exploring it is really a type of energy. We can see this as the energy of consciousness but also our perception of God can be seen as the energy of light. Light is a common metaphor in all mystical spiritual traditions – and we know that ultimately light is vibrational.

We live in a vibrational reality and modern physics is teaching us that as well. When we go beyond the atom to what makes up the components of an atom – beyond protons and electrons – we find it is waves of light and energy, it is vibrational. Our entire physical world is actually waves of light and energy in which the vibrations slow down to become physical matter.

Our consciousness is operating on the highest vibrational level and physics has not been able to measure that but this is a reality that I know, and many others know, to be true. That is the true nature of our consciousness and a truth I have come to accept is that our consciousness precedes our physical reality; consciousness is eternal.

Our consciousness existed before our physical body came into being and then, when we make the choice to take on a physical life, consciousness enters a physical body and becomes attached to that life, that physical manifestation. *We are spiritual beings having a physical experience.*

It is important to understand that all of reality is ultimately vibrational and to understand that consciousness is vibrational energy. As mentioned above, there is no real scientific description or understanding of this energy of consciousness.

If we look at the "computing" power of the brain we can see that the amount of energy there is huge, yet the body only produces small amounts of electrical energy. So exactly how is this amazing amount of energy being produced? Where does the power of our minds come from? The energy of consciousness can thus be determined to be some magnitude of electricity that is way beyond anything that our human mind could produce.

Just think about computers today. The most amazing computers in existence still cannot mimic the human mind in all of its attributes, especially in creativity, and yet they have tremendous computing power and use tremendous amounts of energy. We also know from physics that energy is constant in the universe. That if you destroy something then that energy will just go into another form and that you can not get rid of energy or even matter as that is just a form of energy.

We have this powerful energy that is our conscious awareness. How is it produced? And if we know that energy cannot be lost, what happens to that energy when we die? It is possible that it will just dissipate into the universe because it is already energy of the universe but wouldn't that register somehow? When you take physical matter and destroy it, that energy then becomes something vibrational and it transforms into the energy of heat and/or light, and we can measure that.

But the energy of consciousness is already vibrational so where would it go? It is already a form of energy that is beyond our understanding right now and so what would it turn into – something else that we don't understand?

We do not know how the tremendous energy of consciousness is produced in the first place and we do not know what happens to that energy when we die. Now the metaphysical proposition that consciousness is eternal may seem more reasonable.

In this scenario the energy of consciousness already exists before we are born and that energy continues on when we die. When we die consciousness is no longer tied to that particular tiny stream of human experience that is your current life, but it is still part of the other streams of our experiences and of humanity, our universe and of God.

When this stream of energy that you are experiencing now as your life ends, that stream of consciousness that is experiencing that reality does not go away; it simply moves back into the stream that was all the experiences that you have ever had and it is still part of the larger stream of all of humanity having these experiences. And it is still part of that ocean of consciousness of God's existence.

Our connection to the Divine is consciousness. And it is important to understand that when we decide to manifest in a physical reality, as we mentioned before, our eternal consciousness actually divides itself; one part attaches itself to our human mind and one part remains connected to the eternal. We can call one the thinking or ego mind and the other the divine mind.

The thinking or ego mind is the mind of ideas, thought structures and language and it is what allows you to live the life of a human being. You have to form thoughts and concepts to survive, you need language to talk to other people, and you have to understand the world around you to function and not walk into traffic and to feed yourself.

Over time, starting as a little baby, you develop these thought structures of what is around you.

As you grow these ideas and thoughts become more complex; then people teach you language and you are taught even more ideas, such as what is right and wrong. And thus over time you have created your thinking mind and your ego consciousness.

The energy of the eternal consciousness is still there but it is been sublimated by your thinking mind and these thought patterns, these thought structures which become your ego, the personality of you. And, of course, most of these concepts and thought patterns will actually exist below your conscious awareness, in the subconscious.

We also see that your other mind is the divine mind of God, the eternal continuum that existed before you came into this physical reality and exists after; it is eternal and infinite. As I said earlier, this divine mind has also been called the Soul, the Higher Self and, in Hindu philosophy, the Atman.

But because the thinking mind is always busy, and we are living in that physical plane of the thinking mind, that divine part of your consciousness gets put on the back burner. It is drowned out by our ego mind which always wants to be heard. In a normal human existence many people go through their entire lives without becoming truly aware of that divine aspect of their consciousness. That is

actually the whole point of spiritual awakening –
that you find ways to start to bring that reality of
divine awareness into your everyday awareness
because when you do that it will greatly influence
your ego reality.

What you can see here is that there is sort of a
block to your divine mind – you can look at it as
obstructions to that divine mind. The ego, simply
by its constant creation of thoughts and ideas,
creates these obstructions to your divine nature.

To return to the idea of the energy of consciousness
as light, a common analogy that is used is that there
is a window between your divine mind and your ego
or thinking mind. The intense activity of the ego
mind covers the window, blocking the light of the
Divine and eventually the divine mind is completely
blocked from the every day ego mind.

One thing to stress here, sometimes mistaken by
those on a spiritual path, is that the goal *is never to
eliminate the ego mind.* Our ego mind is what we need
to function in this life. It gives us language and
thoughts, allows us to cross the street safely and
buy groceries so we can eat.

We cannot live permanently in the state of the
divine mind. When I had my experience on the
mountain top my ego self was gone, I was not able

to function as a human being. If I had stayed in that state they would have put me in a mental asylum because I was deliriously happy but I would not have been able to feed myself, I would not have been able to walk or even talk. I would have just been sitting there drooling, a happy drooling idiot but that is not what we came to do in this world, at least not on a continuous basis!

We came into this world to have a human experience, to live and create a human life. We left the divine continuum that we were in, which is pure bliss, to come in here and play the game of being a human being. We cannot be in our divine mind all the time and we cannot even be in there for very long because it is just not a state that fits with what we are here to do as a human being and because the ego mind is very persistent.

But when we touch that divine mind it changes the reality of our existence a little bit by bringing in the love and compassion of the divine mind. And if we can keep having those experiences of our divine mind, even for just a little bit, then over time it begins to permanently change the nature of our ego consciousness. The more experiences we have of connecting to the Divine, the more influence it can have on our overall conscious state.

Most of us spend all of our time locked into our ego structures, our patterns of behavior that have been formed over our lifetime. We are locked into this everyday reality, often with more anxiety or suffering than joy. Once you touch the divine mind and you really start to wake up to the idea that you are in fact this divine creature who is just here having this playful human experience it changes everything, it turns things upside down.

You no longer take your ego consciousness as seriously and you begin to recognize that you are, in fact, creating all of your thoughts including all your anxiety and suffering. When you experience joy however, you are in fact in alignment with your divine mind and this can become the natural state of your ego consciousness as well.

We can see from the above that the thinking mind blocks the divine mind from shining through and shedding divine light on the thinking mind and again light is a common metaphor on how this works. To return to the analogy of the window between our two minds, we saw that all of the thought patterns you form in your life "dirty up" the window.

Eventually the window is so full of thought patterns that no light from the divine mind can shine through. When we clear away the obstructions of our ego selves the window becomes a little clearer and we allow the divine mind to shine through. Spiritual work is then the work of clearing more and more of the window to allow more and more light to shine. What needs to happen is not the elimination of the ego mind but more like the taming of the chatter produced by the ego mind. As we quiet that mind, then the divine mind shines through – and this helps quiet the ego mind even more.

Our connection with the Divine is consciousness. As we experience our human life that connection becomes obscured by our ego self, which is needed to function in a physical time-space reality. The spiritual quest then is to reconnect to our divine aspect, to bring the Divine through, shine that light on our thinking ego mind and to change our reality and lift ourselves out of feeling that we are stuck in a world of unconscious behavior and suffering.

When we see that we actually can gain control of the chattering of our thoughts and feelings, which are all responses to the physical world we inhabit, then we have tremendous power to create a life more in alignment with our Divine Self and this will bring us into a world that is much more joyful and filled with light and love and happiness.

All You Need is Love

One of the key points of coming to a more mature view of God is to understand that God is never angry; God is pure love and the energy of love is what makes up the universe. To go back to our earlier analogy, this means that the rivers and streams of creation we talked about before can be seen as rivers of energy, and that energy can best be described as light that is filled with love.

This is one of those cases where there is no 'scientific' way to prove this. All the great religions teach that God is love. And I can tell you that in those transcendental states I have experienced – *light filled with love* – is the only thing which comes close to describing the energy I was feeling. Thus we will use love as the definition of God's energy.

This love is not the love that we feel in an ego sense – that I love that person or I love my dog, though in that type of love the energy of universal love is still present, any type of love is definitely a taste of that universal energy of love – all the different types of love come from the same source energy of pure universal love. Any time you love somebody, or even love something, that is a positive thing, as you are getting in touch with the energy of love. But the universal love that is in alignment with Divine love is unconditional.

One summer when I was in high school I was working at a camp in Northern Michigan as a lifeguard and swim instructor. I had gone to a local county fair and I saw some jewelry and had an impulse to buy it for my mother.

Like many teens I mostly took my parents for granted. I am pretty sure I had never bought my Mom a present unless it was her birthday, Mother's day or Christmas. When I gave her the jewelry for no reason other than I had thought of her she was floored and actually got tears in her eyes. I had such a feeling of satisfaction and joy – it was a pure moment – and I did not expect or want anything other than to give something to her because I wanted to show her I loved her.

Now, where love can go wrong is with our ego self which then becomes attached to that love and so the love is not freely given. You love someone or something but you want something in return – "I love that person therefore that person must love me and if they don't love me then I'm going to be miserable and unhappy and then I'm going to turn around and hate that person" or "I love ice cream but I want to be able to eat all the ice cream that I can and never gain a pound and if I cannot do that then I'm not happy."

An example of conditional love was as a young man I had a girlfriend I was so in love with that I became a little obsessed with her and afraid that she was not faithful, so I actually ended up driving by her house to spy on her to make sure she was being faithful and loved me as much as I loved her. Needless to say that relationship ended with a lot of pain and I felt embarrassed by my behavior.

When we love with conditions, when we love without any understanding and awareness of how our ego can get in the process then that creates ego based love instead of pure love. But if we can connect to that true energy of love without any conditions then the experience becomes connected to that love which is the underlying energy of the universe.

One way to experience that more universal love is to think about unconditional love you have experienced, such as the love that you have for your children, or the love you have received from your parents. Or to think about the love that you feel watching a beautiful sunset on a beautiful day where everything is at peace and all you feel is this sense of joy and energy and love.

That is the type of love that we are talking about. That is God incarnate. That is the pure nature of God, which is love and this is a very important concept because from that concept it obviously is a non sequitur that you can have an angry God.

Pure love is never angry. When you are angry at someone or something or some situation, you are not in a state of love and - we all know that. We know that when we are angry at the person that we love; then in that moment we are not feeling that love. Hopefully we are connected enough to our love for that person that it does not last very long, but in that moment of anger, love has gone away.

Since God is eternal and infinite, and is eternal love and infinite love, then there is simply no place for anger there, it just cannot exist. It does not make sense to say that God is infinite love and then turn around and say that "God is angry" because you did something.

The idea of an angry God is again a case of humans transferring human attributes to the infinite. We imagine that God must have human attributes and therefore God can be angry. This goes in hand with God then making rules and becoming angry when those rules are broken.

God Does Not Make Rules

When I was fifteen years old I had an experience that ended my time with the Episcopal church. The Episcopal church does not have an individual confession like the Catholic church, but at that time it had a general confession where everyone got on their knees and you are all praying and telling God what a terrible sinner you are and how unworthy you are to be there in God's presence.

Well this particular Sunday morning it was at a time when the previous week I had received the Eagle Boy Scout award. At that same time I was also on the school swim team. Basically all I did was go to school and then go to swim practice and then go home and do homework, watch TV and go to bed. I did some Scouting stuff on the weekends and that was it.

Now I found myself on a Sunday morning on my knees telling God what a horrible sinner I was and I started thinking – you know I'm not really doing anything bad here, how am I such a horrible sinner? It just really did not ring true to me. And I stopped going to church.

It is very important that we come to a new understanding of the true nature of God because it is the old structure that does much of the damage in the world. It is the old structure of an entity that is sitting up there in judgment, an entity that has made rules that we must follow, an entity that determines who is good and who is bad and who goes to heaven and who goes to hell.

That old structure also creates much of the anger and frustration and animosity towards other people in the world. If you believe that you have a God who has created rules and everybody must follow them, then of course you are going to be inclined to be very negative towards people who do not follow those rules. You are going to see them as not worthy, that they are in fact not in accordance with God and therefore why should they get any kind of consideration whatsoever.

You may even be angry at them and wish them harm; after all they are defying God in your eyes. And of course often these spiritual rules will be created, interpreted and upheld by some organized group. That is what has brought us to the type of fundamentalist religious groups that we have today, where they think that their version of God is the one and only way and therefore their version of the rules that they think God has laid down are correct, and anyone who does not follow those rules is outside of God's love.

But the reality is that God does not make rules – ever. Human beings are the ones who make rules because God is beyond our reality and the only way God can be perceived in our reality is as pure love and compassion.

This idea that God does not make rules goes even further when we understand that from a divine point of view there is no right or wrong. This is a very difficult concept for people to get because we all see things that seem very bad, things that we would say are evil and yet God is pure love so these things must be against God. But if we accept the fact that God has created everything then we also must accept that God has created that which we say is evil. What explains this contradiction – something seems to be bad, not loving at all but it is still part of God?

Here we return to the understanding that all of our existence, and especially our consciousness, is vibrational. The highest vibrational level is our Divine Self – which is a direct emanation of God. Our thinking or ego mind exists at different lower vibrational levels. Different thought patterns will either be pointing us toward the Divine and be of a higher vibration, and others will be heading away from the Divine and can be seen as lower vibrations.

Some may think at this point that we are just playing with words. That we are saying from an absolute view there is no right or wrong but then replacing it with this concept of vibrational levels which seems to be the same thing as right versus wrong. But the very important part of this is that there is no divine judgment involved. There can be human judgment but God never judges. From that divine point of view a lower vibrational level is not wrong, it just is. We can say it is less desirable but that is subjective.

While there is no right or wrong from a divine perspective, there are patterns of thought that lead us away from the energy of God, and the energy of universal divine love, and patterns that lead us towards that energy.

When we see someone who has done something horrible, someone who has killed or raped, someone whose actions have caused much suffering to other human beings, we have to understand that from a pure divine sense that person still has the same Divine Being within them that we all have, and that is not going to change.

But from within their human experience they are moving further and further away from their own divine state and are causing much suffering to others, as well as tremendous suffering to themselves.

That is the way that consciousness works. The further away from your divine nature you are, the more suffering you will experience. People who do these horrible things, even though they may seem like they are happy or it may even seem like they get pleasure out of these terrible activities, you have to understand that what we hear or see of them is a tiny blip of their ongoing existence. Internally, their consciousness will manifest as terrible suffering; for them the world is not a place filled with love, and they are not connected to others or to their Divine Self.

This is not a state of happiness; this is not a state of someone who is experiencing joy. This is a state of someone who is suffering tremendously and in turn they cause suffering in others – especially if those others do not have the awareness to mitigate that suffering.

This state is not connected to the pure energy of God that is within all of us. This is someone as a human being strongly attached to their human thought structures and their ego consciousness and deeply removed from their divine nature. To go back to the window analogy – for people living this type of reality the window is boarded up and no divine light ever shines through.

The negative patterns that lead to this type of suffering and acting out are almost always created when people are young children. This is why children raised in abusive homes often turn out to be abusive later on. Because these youngsters have been raised without love they form which block the divine love within them and they are pushed further and further away from their Divine Self. This is why raising children in a loving and supportive way should be a top priority for everyone in society.

Of course there are cases where people raised in a loving way still may end up doing things that we see as wrong, or in our terms, take them away from the divine within. These are people who may have come into this world with "negative" structures or tendencies from previous lives. Or they created those structures in this lifetime even with a loving upbringing, but luckily the number of people who fall into these categories is relatively small.

As a society we can certainly try to control what we deem to be negative behavior, we can certainly say this is not behavior that we accept and that, if necessary, we are going to take those people away and lock them up to punish them. That is part of what we as human beings need to do to have a human society. But from a pure divine standpoint there is no right or wrong, there is just existence, there are just people acting out as being people. This is important because we have to understand that as human beings we are the ones that determine right and wrong and we are the ones that make rules.

While we certainly have the right and even the obligation to set boundaries for what is right in society, we cannot say that these are divine rules. God is not dictating these rules, man is making these rules. And the truth is that even religions which do believe they have the inside track on God's rules recognize the relative nature of those rules. Thus we have the case where the commandment is "thou shall not kill" yet we allow that people in the military can kill or that it is ok to kill in self defense.

Another obvious example of the fallacy of God making rules is the arguments that many people in fundamentalist religions make against homosexuality. They have determined that it is God's "rule" that a certain way of living is the right way and therefore they can make up rules against other people who are not living that way.

God does not make any rules about anybody living any way, or about sex. And the fact is that if any two people love each other, they are totally and completely in alignment with divine love. They are moving towards the divine energy of love, they are moving towards the love that underlies the entire creation and anybody who is blocking that or condemning that as "wrong" is in fact moving away from God, moving away from the love that is the divine nature of God.

It is very important to understand this concept of moving away from your divine nature and moving towards your divine nature. We can then see our behavior towards others in that light. We don't need rules; we can simply ask the question – "Is this leading me towards my Divine Self? Do I feel joy and happiness, am I inspiring joy and happiness in other people, am I connecting to the great consciousness that we all share, am I lighter? "

Here again the use of the idea of light comes back into the picture. But in this context it is the feeling of lightness. When you do things that are "right" you feel lighter – you are vibrating at a higher level. You have a sense of happiness about you. When you do things that are not "right" you feel heavier, it weighs on you, and your vibrational reality is slower. You can see it as guilt, your guilty conscience weighing you down or as having a heavy heart. These are all terms that we use and they are true because it is actually the weight of your consciousness versus the lightness of your consciousness.

God is never angry, God does not make rules, and God is love. We as human beings can and should make rules for our society, for our common good in living together, but we have to understand that these are rules that we make up and that these rules are never rules from God, because God is beyond our finite world.

Our Freedom to Create

Understanding that God does not make rules brings up the question – why did God create this reality where people can go down a path away from their Divine Self and do things that we perceive as bad, things that, as we talked about before, weigh down their consciousness and create suffering? What we have to understand is that our free will is the key to our human existence. Free will is the key to our being able to create a human life.

Free will allows us to go forward into the world and create an existence, which is the whole point of God manifesting here through us. We are God experiencing itself. We are God having a human experience through our consciousness.

If our whole life was predetermined, if it was all set in stone when we came here, then there would be no energy of creation. There would be really no purpose in our existence, it would be all known before we came forward. The whole purpose of coming forward into a human life is to expand that creation, to have experiences that allow the joy of this creation to manifest.

Some people believe that our lives are predetermined, in a sense, by our karma. Karma is the concept that our actions in a previous life will influence who we are and what happens to us in our current life. For me karma makes sense because it relates back to the idea that all of consciousness, and all of our existence, is vibrational. If you had some very strong vibrational patterns in a previous lifetime, then to me it is logical that those vibrational patterns may leave a resonance that will be there when you decide to come back into a physical reality.

This also ties back to our river and stream analogy. This stream of consciousness we are experiencing now is connected to a larger stream which is all the lives we have ever lived. So if you create an especially strong vibrational pattern in one life it may create a resonance in other lifetimes. However, I also believe that the vibrational patterns you create in you current lifetime are far more powerful that any previous life patterns.

It is what we do in this lifetime, the experiences that we have in this lifetime that will shape us much more than these past lifetimes. It is free will that allows us to break the chains of karmic structures, both previous lifetime patterns and current lifetime patterns, and to get back in touch with our divine nature and then go forward to create in a whole new way.

Even when we are creating out of the structures or patterns that have happened in this lifetime or being influenced by previous lifetimes, it is still free will that allows us to go forward and create even when the starting point is coming from those structures. That is an important point to understand; that we have this free will and that is why we can make these choices that either takes us towards being aligned with Divine Consciousness or takes us away from that alignment.

Even though I do believe in the concept of karma I do not believe that just because you did something bad in a previous life that means that you are going to have the exact opposite happen to you in this lifetime.

To me this concept of karma implies that you are punished for bad deeds which would imply that God is punishing you. That would be God making rules and, as we discussed before, God does not do that.

This also means that there is no heaven and hell. That was also one of the things that led me away from my church as a teenager. It made no sense to me that what we do in the space of a 70 year life would then result in an eternity of damnation – that idea always seemed like a very unloving God to me.

The same thing is true about karma. The idea that if you do "bad things" in this lifetime, that you are going to come back and suffer in the next lifetime, is really no different than the idea of going to hell for sins you commit. The only real difference is that in the concept of hell damnation is eternal and in the concept of karma you can work your way out of the bad karmic situation, but in both cases it is still a punishing God.

However, it seems reasonable to me that if you do some "bad" things in this lifetime it may create a pattern, a vibrational pattern that might be a match to vibrational patterns when you come back in a future life. If you were making others suffer in a certain way perhaps you will suffer in a similar fashion in a future life because you have set up a vibrational pattern that you are sensitive to and which creates a match in another incarnation.

It is not God punishing you but simply the metaphysics of the vibrational reality. But as we discussed earlier, your free will always allow you to break any of these vibrational patterns. You are not doomed to suffer from karma any more then you are doomed to go to hell. And it should be noted that these same metaphysical laws would apply to the reverse; the positive things you do will set up vibrational matches for future good things to happen.

The Human Condition

We established earlier that our consciousness, our eternal Divine Consciousness, separates into two aspects to live a human life. One aspect is the divine mind which is eternal, infinite, pure joy, pure love and it is, in fact, a part of God. There is no separation between our Divine Consciousness and God consciousness; they are one and the same.

The other aspect of consciousness becomes our human thinking or ego mind and this is the mind that we live with everyday. It is the ego mind that allows us to be human beings and it is important that we understand that the thought structures formed by our ego mind allow us to have a human experience but at the same time these structures also get in the way of our being in touch with our divine mind.

The easiest way to see this is to see that a baby comes into this life with no structures and no ability to take care of itself. Not only physically, but it has no ability to say or do anything. A baby's consciousness is pure divine energy. The thinking mind simply expresses itself, when it wants something it cries and when it is happy it laughs. As the baby develops, the thinking mind develops; at first the baby cannot even make out shapes. It has no depth perception; it has no structures about anything.

As time goes by the baby becomes a child and the child develops structures. The child learns shapes, it learns depth perception, it learns physical touch, sight, sound, smell, all the senses start to create structures that it begins to recognize. Of course this is also happening along with physical developments of the brain and body as the baby grows.

Over time there is a learning process. The baby has to learn that hot things burn it, how to walk and talk, etc. and all of these different lessons that it learns create thought patterns or thought structures that are stored in the human mind, the human consciousness. The child builds up these basic thought patterns and then it learns more abstract thought structures such as telling the truth and what love is and what is beauty, happiness, etc., etc.

It is important to understand that the every day reality that we perceive is all based on these thought patterns. These thought patterns or thought structures are the building blocks that give our lives structure. In a very real sense there is no reality until we create it by our perceptions and the thought patterns we then attach to those perceptions. We create reality from thought patterns and as we create the same patterns again and again our lives have continuity. And as we all create similar thought structures we seem to share a common reality.

Everybody agrees that a table is a table and a chair is a chair and there is general consensus on things, what is right and wrong in society, etc., but even though we have a basic agreement we are all experiencing slightly different perceptions of these common realities. It is always our own structures that we use to translate the energy of things around us into things we recognize.

We see something because we recognize the light coming at us, the energy coming at us, the senses then perceive that energy and we translate that to say this is X and this is Y, this is good, this is bad. All of that is created based on these thought patterns and the older we get the more thought patterns we store and it makes our ego self, our thinking mind, denser in a way.

Children are seen as "lighter" because in fact they have fewer of these thought structures. They are more spontaneous, they are interacting with the world in a different way than we are because they do not have all of these thought patterns.

The older we are the more thought structures we have stored and thus our ego mind becomes hardened, or another term often used is that it becomes "crystallized". One of the steps to understanding the nature of our ego mind and then learning how to quiet our ego chatter is to learn to recognize these thought patterns.

This is where the concept of karma comes back into play. A lot of people think about karma in terms of past lives and we discussed that earlier. But I think the real point of karma is not worrying about past lives but the karma of the experiences that you have in this life.

For example, imagine as a child I was bullied by somebody with red hair and up to that point I had no experience with anybody with red hair. Now I have had an experience with somebody with red hair and they were mean to me and they beat me up and they made me miserable and I suffered because of that person with red hair.

I may unconsciously then have a negative reaction to people with red hair. It will not necessarily come out in a manifestation where I run away from somebody with red hair but there will be a subtle dislike when I first meet someone, or I will be predisposed to not like them.

That is the karma of this lifetime. That is a hidden negative thought structure that I am not aware of; that is what real karma is. If that happened to me once and then I met a red haired girl and fell in love with her than maybe I would not have that same thought pattern. But if I met three people with red hair and every single one of them was mean and nasty to me then I probably would form some sort of thought pattern below the surface, not something that I was aware of, that would make me not like red haired people.

This is a very important concept because that is the type of karma that we have to deal with to help us quiet our ego chatter. That is karma – the unconscious predisposition to liking or not liking things based on previous thought patterns that we have established.

The strongest obstructions to getting in touch with the divine mind are deep-seated negative karmic patterns that keep us in our ego state, and since these are negative patterns they are tied to suffering. We are using the term negative here not as a judgment but simply to distinguish patterns of thought that are unpleasant and create the negative emotions of anger, hatred, greed, jealousy, etc.

This is why even people who do a lot of spiritual work often wonder why are they still reliving certain patterns. They know the Divine exists; they even have had wonderful experiences of the divine state of consciousness. Why are they not in a happier state all the time, why do they still end up doing things that makes them suffer or why do they end up in another failed relationship?

The answer is always in the ego thought structures they have created. It is the karmic patterns that they have established in this lifetime. Again, there may be some influence from previous lifetimes or other forces but the main karmic structures are going to be the experiences that they have had in this lifetime and that is the blockage which is what keeps us all in a cycle of suffering.

It is what keeps you from experiencing more of the joy of divine energy even if you have had a taste of it. Certainly before you begin on the spiritual path and really start to work on these ego structures, these structures are going to keep you blocked from your divine energy.

I do not want to sugar coat the process that is needed here. When you first begin on this path of self discovery and awareness and understanding you are going to have to face these deep seated negative ego patterns and it is not always a pleasant thing to do.

It is a painful lesson when you see the suffering that these patterns are creating in yourself, and perhaps even helping to create in others, if they allow that. And it is a lesson that you have to learn over and over as you uncover more of these patterns and even rework the same patterns. That is why spiritual work is called working on your self. It is literally work to go in there and dig into these patterns.

Our True Nature

I want to talk a little bit here about what is referred to as our true nature. True nature refers to the natural state of a human being who does not have any ego patterns blocking them from the Divine. Many spiritual teachers say that our true nature is a state of joy which is completely true in the absolute terms of the divine mind.

The divine mind is pure consciousness, pure joy, pure love and our ego thinking mind can be a reflection of that divine mind. But I think there is a kind of subtle caveat here, and that is that in our thinking mind the natural state is not joy. The natural state is neutrality, or what is often referred to as emptiness.

The best way to look at that is again to look at a baby. A baby is born into this world with no structures at all and is in a sense an empty vessel. It is just a pure human consciousness when it first comes in to this physical plane and it is still reflecting the Divine, which we see in the joy a baby experiences, but it will also immediately begin to experience negativity.

No one teaches the baby to cry, that is an automatic human response. Sometimes when the baby first comes into the world the first thing it is doing is crying but certainly if not the first thing then very soon after the baby will experience a state of discomfort about something. Their diapers need changing or they are hungry or they are colicky or whatever, and the baby will cry. The baby will express the unhappiness it is feeling. There is no attachment to that unhappiness just as there is no attachment to the happiness. You can see that very clearly.

A baby can be giggling and laughing and then two seconds later be crying. It does not hold on to either state of being. It goes back and forth from one state to another purely on what it feels in that moment.

When we understand that, when we see clearly that there is no attachment to joy and happiness or to sadness and unhappiness, we can see that the baby's mind is really neutral. That is in fact the human consciousness as the baby first manifests in our physical reality.

At first the baby will just experience whatever is going on around it without any filters. It is collecting input and then reacting to what is going on. What happens as we grow older is that we become more attached to the suffering side than the happiness side. Now, why would we do something as silly as that? Well, as with all of our thought patterns, we are sort of trained into doing that.

If we go back to the example of a baby, when the baby is happy the parents maybe are paying attention to it but they may not really pay much attention. The baby is sitting there in the crib, happy, and the parents are taking care of other things and they see the baby is happy so they leave it alone.

Now, when the baby becomes unhappy what happens? Immediately the parents are going to pay attention to it. The baby starts crying and the parents are going to go over and see what's wrong and take care of the baby. As we said before, our thinking ego mind is creating thought patterns all the time, therefore one of the very first thought patterns that will be created is that being unhappy and upset is rewarded with attention from those around us.

We all know this goes on throughout our lives. If a child throws a temper tantrum often someone is going to pay some attention to him or her. And that is why it is very important to not indulge children in their temper tantrums because you are in fact just really reinforcing a thought pattern that if they act out they are going to get attention. Nevertheless, as we get older the tendency is that people pay attention to us when we are suffering, when we are unhappy, when we are depressed, even when we are angry.

As young adults and teenagers and on into adulthood, people are going to pay attention to us when we are in a negative state; there is a lot of energy around that kind of suffering. This is reflected in society where there is a lot of art geared towards people who are suffering – poetry and movies and music – all of which reinforces the idea of suffering as being important, or noble, or growth inducing.

The other aspect of this is that over time our thinking mind will come to see our negative patterns as its power base. When we move closer to our divine mind we reduce our suffering and in a sense our thinking mind loses some of its power.

The thinking or ego mind has a natural state of existence that it wants to keep and the more that we suffer the more our thinking mind has a hold over us. The happier we are, the more joyful we are and we are much more in touch with the energy of our divine mind which then starts to play a larger role in our existence. This is why spiritual work in some traditions is actually depicted as a battle between your minds; however that is a more advanced spiritual conversation, and we will table that for the purposes of this book.

Over time we become used to states of anxiety, discontentment and suffering and this was the Buddha's great insight – that human existence becomes attached to suffering or discontentment. He saw that the nature of our existence becomes suffering because we are always in a state of desire or attachment. We want things. If we do not get what we want then we suffer. If we do get what we want then we are afraid of losing it or it is are not as good as we hoped for, and in that sense we are suffering as well.

The Buddha saw that in this way all human consciousness becomes attached to its suffering and discontentment. He realized that it is only by giving up on desire and releasing our attachments that we can escape that suffering. We have to learn to empty our mind of this desire and attachment. We have to be able to return to our original neutral state, to become an empty vessel again.

This goes along with the idea above that we are trained to suffer. That we are encouraged to suffer and that our suffering then becomes a powerful force that our ego mind wants to hold on to. How to change that? Well, that gets into our next chapter; Divine Self.

Divine Self

We saw in the previous chapter that the natural state of our thinking mind is to be neutral but that over time it evolves into a state of attachment and dissatisfaction. That is the human condition for the great majority of people, and if they do not do any spiritual work, their life may be filled with suffering, anxiety and discontent.

They will certainly experience joy and pleasure but they will often spend more time in a state of some sort of dissatisfaction which can be defined as being afraid, anxious, worried, angry, sad or depressed – all these different terms that we have to describe our negative states. And in fact many people currently spend a majority of their time in those states of dissatisfaction.

How do we break those dissatisfactions? We break them by getting back in touch with our Divine Self. When spiritual teachers talk about our true nature as being joy, what they are talking about is the natural state of our divine mind, that part of our consciousness which is eternal, which existed before we came in to live this life and which exists after this life. Our divine mind is our direct connection to our Divine Self.

The natural state of our thinking mind is neutrality or emptiness. Emptiness does not necessarily mean an absence of thoughts, though that would be the highest manifestation of that state. But as we saw earlier, that would be impossible to maintain on a regular basis. Emptiness here means empty of attachments to our patterns and, as much as possible, empty of our negative patterns and emotions. This allows you to face reality freshly and innocently without a lot of preconceived thought structures.

The way to get to a neutral or empty state is to quiet your mind of the constant chatter that normally goes on. If we can learn to quiet the ego mind then two things occur. First, we begin to respond to things that happen to us from a more neutral state, without all the subconscious thought patterns that prejudice us and drive our behavior. Secondly, we allow the energy of the divine mind to come forward more, which does provide us with a sense of joy and expanding love which will also influence how we respond to life's events.

Again, in the previous chapter when we mentioned that many spiritual teachers say our natural state is joy – this is what is meant. If we can tame our ego mind that is full of chatter, then the divine mind begins to flood us with the infinite joy and compassion of divine energy. We also become more expansive in our view of the world and those around us.

Putting your ego mind into a more neutral state and getting in touch with your divine mind on an ongoing basis means you need to form some sort of ongoing meditative practice. You need to have some type of practice that allows you to quiet the thinking mind for some small period of time which will allow your divine mind to begin to shine through the window a little bit more.

It is only through some sort of meditative practice that you can quiet your mind. Meditation does not necessarily mean sitting and doing an actual formal practice, though I personally find that has the best results. It is my experience that people who do a more formal practice, such as Buddhist meditation, have the best results. I believe this is because this type of structured practice makes it easier to stick with an ongoing schedule.

However even simply sitting quietly every day for 15 minutes could produce positive results. Prayer is also certainly a form of meditative practice. Even singing and dancing can be used in a meditative way to connect you back to your Divine Self.

I will discuss mediation in more detail in a later chapter but the key point here is that meditation is a necessary step to quiet the thinking mind and allow the divine mind to shine more brightly.

There is also another way to get in touch with your Divine Self which is the use of certain psychoactive drugs, which for some, may induce a transcendental experience or something close to it. We live in a culture in which these drugs are illegal. And unfortunately any drug can be abused, so I am not advocating that people take this path.

But it is a fact that if guided properly many who have taken a "trip" have had a positive and even profound experience which opened them up to new possibilities. Hopefully in the future we will be able to approach this topic with a balance between society's needs and individual freedom.

It is definitely not the long term answer, however. My experiences on hallucinogens were very powerful but they did not match the transcendental experiences I had when I was not on any sort of drugs.

The pure transcendental experience that comes from going beyond your normal consciousness in an awakened natural state is the most powerful and long lasting experience. But the transcendental experience of hallucinogens can give you the taste that makes it easier to start down the road of discovering your true nature.

Reading various spiritual teachings can also be a way to learn how to see the process of your ego mind versus your divine mind. For those people who are inclined to read and understand spirituality on an intellectual level you can get quite a bit out of reading about different spiritual traditions and it can open up your mind to seeing things in a different way. However, since all intellectual activity is part of the thinking mind you will still need some other type of practice to clear the window between the thinking mind and the divine mind.

Is That You God?

If God is in us all of the time, and we are always connected to God, then it would seem to lead to the idea that we can speak to God or God can speak to us and tell us what to do. The answer to that is yes and no.

As we established before, there are two aspects to our consciousness – one that is eternal and divine and one that becomes our ego personality. The fact is that our ego personality so totally dominates our consciousness that we rarely "hear" the Divine within us unless we spend some amount of time developing that ability. And even when we do develop the ability to quiet our minds and to get into a state where we can experience divine energy – those experiences are relatively brief.

But it is true that your Divine Consciousness is always present. The way that it will manifest is in your intuition. We are often told to listen to your "gut" or to go with your first instinct. What this really means is that you have access to knowledge that is beyond your thinking mind's structures. Your divine mind is aware of what is going on in your life and will provide you with information and direction but it is not going not be in the form of words or even a clear concise thought. It will be in the form of a feeling.

We must always remember that *words, thoughts and ideas are always a part of the ego personality.* Even when you have a strong experience of the Divine you will then try to translate that into normal thoughts and words but this translation is now subject to the filters and structures of your mind. The Divine within us is energy and that energy can influence our mind and our ego personality, but it can not speak to us directly in words; divine energy is beyond words.

We have discussed earlier the idea that there is a window between the thinking ego mind and the divine mind. As long as we are experiencing a physical life this window will be there and it will obscure the divine mind. Even the most dedicated meditation practitioner will not permanently clear all thoughts from their mind.

You might even have moments of pure awareness, but that experience is beyond words. We can see that in our normal lives the divine light shining through the window, which in a sense would be God talking to you, will always be filtered and somewhat blocked. When you hear words in your head they are your words, not God's.

But what will happen is that the more time you spend quieting the ego mind and allowing the divine light to shine through, the more it will change your ego mind on a permanent basis. The effects of quieting the mind become more permanent the more you practice. In addition, your intuition will become a stronger force for guidance.

Remember it is all vibrational, the more you bring the vibrations of the divine mind into your thinking mind the more you will change the vibrational level of your thinking mind. As this divine light affects you it does change your thoughts and ideas, your outlook on the world.

The Divine will always speak to you through your intuition and it can influence your thoughts. Even though the Divine will never speak directly to you in words, the more you work to quiet your thinking mind and allow the divine mind to shine through, the more it will become a positive and permanent part of your ongoing outlook on life.

Finding Your Path

If you have gotten this far in the book hopefully you are now interested in finding a way on the path to self awareness. Or perhaps you have already started on that path and you are looking to go deeper in your journey. It may even be that you are not happy with the path you currently are on and want to try a different path. In this chapter we will talk a little bit about finding your way on your path and the first and most important point is that *it is always your path, you must take full responsibility for yourself.*

There is not a single way that you must follow to get to your divine nature. Your divine nature exists within you. It is always there, it is just waiting to shine and the purpose in following a particular spiritual path is simply to find one that resonates with you and that can give you some tools that allow your Divine Self to shine through.

The first and most important point is to always listen to your intuition, your inner self. Your Divine Self will help guide you through your intuition. It is your inner guide.

If something feels right try it out and if it does not feel right, stop. Always go with your intuition because it may very well be the case that something is not right for you now but it will be right for you later.

If it was right for you it should feel right immediately. If you come across a spiritual teaching and think that it looks interesting, but then you go to a meeting or class and it does not feel right, then back off for the moment. You can explore something else or keep reading about that tradition or try a different meeting or class with a different group, whatever seems right, but keep listening to your intuition, your inner guide.

The other thing that goes along with this idea is that not all teachers are right for all seekers. There are many different spiritual paths one can pursue. For example, there are teachings which approach the spiritual from a more emotional or heart centered standpoint. In my case I have studied with the Sufi tradition and their tradition is all about love and it is all about opening your heart.

Their teachings are heart-centered and are all about being joyful and experiencing God's love. If that type of teaching resonates with your nature then that that path might be something that will appeal to you. I had a great experience working in that tradition and it meant a lot to me while I was doing it but ultimately I was more attracted to my Arica path which was a little bit more intellectual. It just had a different feel and energy to it and that was what resonated with me. Buddhism would be another example of something that tends to be more intellectual in the way it approaches the spiritual path.

The point is that there are many ways and no one way is right for everybody. There is a famous saying, "When the student is ready the master will appear," and that goes back to this idea that you will find your way when you are ready. Do not force it, do not push it.

However, the flip side of listening to your intuition is that you will also most likely have to overcome your ego resistance even if your intuition is saying that something is good, or appeals to you. It is a subtle thing but you have to be able to distinguish between when your whole intuition, your whole being, is telling you this does not feel right, versus when your ego gets in the way and starts to analyze things and throws up roadblocks. Your ego will say, "I like doing this but I do not have the time to do this." Or "I like doing this but this teacher has red hair and I do not like people with red hair" - to go back to our previous example.

You have to be able to distinguish between ego resistance and intuition because, as we discussed before, your thinking ego self is always going to put up resistance to you becoming more aware because that is lessening the power that your ego self has; the ego self definitely holds on to it's power, that is just a fact of consciousness.

We all get stuck in certain patterns, ego thought patterns that we become comfortable with. They are familiar, and even if the pattern is unpleasant it is still in a sense comfortable because it is familiar, and your ego mind is not going to let go of that "comfortable" pattern. It is an important lesson to remember – your ego will hold onto suffering because it is a familiar pattern. When trying to grow and change you will always to have to overcome this ego resistance.

Also it is a good idea to always keep your mind open to other sources of knowledge and practice. It is dangerous to get into a situation where you are in a group or on some spiritual path which teaches or believes it is the only way to be connected to God. This is the danger of fundamentalism in religion and is never the truth because there are many paths to the Divine. There is no single path and anybody who says their way is the only way that you can reach divine awareness is wrong because that goes back to a concept of God that is completely wrong.

God did not create one way, God did not lay down rules that say you must do this practice or you must think this way to get in touch with your divine nature. If you are in a group that claims that their way is the only way, get out, period.

The best way to avoid a cult or ego-based gurus is to make sure that you are not in a situation where they demand your total obedience. You should be suspicious of any teacher that does not say "question everything, including me."

You always should be allowed to question your teacher. Even once you are on a path and are committed to following a certain tradition or working with a teacher and everything seems wonderful, you still need to always maintain your self awareness and to make sure that what you are learning rings true. Your teacher always deserves respect but never blind loyalty. Here again, you must always be listening to your inner guide.

If you are in a group that is demanding complete loyalty, complete subservience to their way then again – get out. You may have had a positive experience up until then, but those positive experiences will be limited and long term you will simply create a new set of very strong ego-based thought patterns that will actually block you from your divine mind.

Many cults or groups that are ego-driven still have some good teachings that they pass on to their students, especially if someone is just starting on the spiritual path. The basic teachings of a lot of these groups are common to many other groups in that they may teach you some basic spiritual truths, like recognizing the difference between your ego self and your Divine Self, which are positive teachings.

But they then take that energy and create a new ego structure around it that demands loyalty only to them and that is where the danger is. Instead of your ego losing power over you, this group's teachings will create in you a new rigid ego structure – an ego structure which believes that there is one and only one path to the Divine. They may even instruct that you cannot talk to anybody else or see your family along with other authoritarian rules that have no place in a true spiritual path.

As stated before, you do not have to join any group; however, I do think it is difficult to be on the spiritual path all on your own. As I discussed earlier I went through a period where I was quite "anti-group" and thought the best spiritual path was to do it yourself. I have since found that working with a group will greatly accelerate your progress. To learn meditation practices, and other skills in overcoming your ego resistance, there is usually a need to be in some sort of supportive community that can help you on your path, even if it is only temporary, even if you only attend some seminars here and there. But the best and fastest way to progress along the spiritual path is to find an on-going support group that resonates with you.

There are many different paths available. We have talked about Buddhism, the Sufi tradition and others. The Christian tradition has a mystical side to it. You do not have to be locked into a fundamentalist Christian view to call yourself a Christian no matter what any church might say. The Sufi tradition is the mystical side of the Islamic religion. Hinduism obviously has the yoga tradition.

There are modern schools like the Arica School founded by Oscar Ichazo. George Gurdjieff was a Russian mystic of the early 20th century whose teachings still have followers. There are also enneagram studies which were actually originally taken from the Arica School and the teachings of Oscar Ichazo. It is my belief that some of the people who are working with enneagram teachings are mistaken in their approach. However some, like A.H. Almaas, have worked with the enneagram in a way that has evolved into, or added on to, their own spiritual practice. Many of the people who work with the Law of Attraction, such as my friend Eva Gregory, also have a very strong spiritual aspect to their work and teachings.

These are all paths, different ways that you can look at spirituality. These spiritual paths will have appeal to some and not to others. If you approach any of these ways with the understanding of the true nature of God then they can all enrich and enhance your experience. If you approach any of those with the idea that this is the one and the only way then, as we discussed, that is a danger.

I need to say a word on organized religions. You need to be clear that there is a difference between spiritual teachings and an institutional religion. When a religion becomes an institution, a part of society, with its own rules, regulations and hierarchy then that is an aspect of the thinking mind, not the divine mind.

Much of the activity of the institution moves from spiritual teachings to maintaining the institution. The original spiritual teachings may even become obscured by the people running the institution. Over time this tendency can become more embedded and instead of teaching people how to experience more light, to awaken to their true nature, they are in fact creating more ego structures and blockage to the divine mind.

However, in most cases the original spiritual teachings are still part of the religion and you can find people and teachers in any religion that will still be letting the Divine light through. Being involved in a religion can also give you a sense of community. There is nothing wrong with being involved with a religion but you must take responsibility for your own spiritual growth.

Always remember that nothing stands between you and God – you always have a direct connection and it is not dependent on any religion, teachings or teacher.

Hopefully this brief overview will assist you in finding and getting started on your path. As you start out, I would advise that you try different teachings to see what resonates with you. I have also included at the end of this book a list of a few books that I believe can give you a sense of some of the different paths I have written about.

Practicing Compassion

One practice that many traditions and religions share is learning to practice compassion towards anyone we meet or are involved with. Practicing compassion is a universal exercise because the energy of love and compassion is in direct alignment with the fundamental nature of God. Compassion, which is a form of universal love, in this context is the understanding of the divine nature of all human beings and it is the feeling of connection that we can have to all human beings, and in fact to all living things on our planet and in our universe, including the Earth itself.

The more compassion that we can practice, the more that we are able to get in alignment with our true divine self, our true divine love. This must be a sincere practice and must come from a real desire within. It cannot come from a sense of obligation or be forced.

In other words, if you think – well I am going to be compassionate because my teacher ordered me to be compassionate – that is not real compassion. It has to be something that you nurture and develop where, for example, you get in touch with how you feel and what you are experiencing when you do feel compassion for somebody – just learn to hold onto that for a minute and feel what that is like and see if you can expand it. Or you can even see it in the negative, see when you lack compassion and learn from that.

When I took refuge in the Kagyu Buddhist lineage I was given a Tibetan name. My name translated as "Ever Pure Patience". At first I thought that was because I had always seen myself as a patient guy. It was only after I got the name that I realized how truly impatient I was.

One time, years ago, I was waiting in line at a grocery store in the express lane which was not moving at all. I saw there was someone upfront who I could not see clearly and she seemed to be taking forever. I made some comment out loud about holding up the line. Right after that the woman finished and stepped away and I saw she was a little old lady, who was at least 80 and was using a cane. I wanted to disappear into the floor. What a total cad I had been. Because I was held up for all of 5 minutes I had wanted to make her feel bad. It was a strong lesson in the need to always be practicing compassion, as well as patience.

A good way to develop this practice is when you do feel an unconditional love for someone, like your child, see if you can expand that to other children and realize that their parents have that same love for them and then feel a connection and compassion for the parents. Even if you think the other child is a little bit of a brat and you are thinking that you are glad you are not their parent, you can still feel how the parent loves that child. And you can feel compassion for the parents and how they love their difficult child.

You can nurture and develop this compassion, not from a sense of obligation, but from the sense of taking whatever love you already are experiencing and then just expand it. Try to hold on to that feeling a little bit more. It is an easy exercise to practice if you pay attention to your feelings.

Another way to do this exercise is to try feeling compassion for someone you do not like. Think about them in a different way. For example you have an office mate who really annoys you. See if there is something about them that you can identify with to see them in a different way. Maybe they have pictures of their children on their desk, and then you can think of them as a loving parent.

At work they are annoying the hell out of you but you now see that they go home and they are a loving parent. And now you recognize they have that love in them and their children love them so that maybe now you have a little bit more compassion for them.

Also a great way to practice compassion is to understand what we have discussed earlier in that people who are acting out negatively are in fact suffering more. That person who is being nasty has an internal reality which is suffering much more than what you are experiencing. Remember, our reality is dictated by our consciousness. Someone who is angry, mean, or nasty is living with that state all the time. You only experience them for a brief period and you never have to experience that negative reality if you choose not to.

You can now feel compassion for that person, you can feel compassion for the fact that they are suffering. Rather than seeing their nastiness and thinking what a nasty person they are and how you do not like them, see them and think – "oh that's a nasty person and they are really suffering living in that state much of their time." You do not feel pity – you just recognize their suffering and feel compassion for them. This does not mean you need to be friends with them, it just means you see them in a different light – which changes your reality.

Right there you have changed the dynamics, you have opened yourself up more, you are experiencing compassion and the benefit for you is that person and their negativity does not affect you as much. Their nastiness is no longer bringing you down and making you feel negative. It is now transformed – or transmuted – into a feeling of compassion. The more that you can practice that the more it will become second nature to you. You may also find in some cases it will actually change the other person and they will become less negative to you as a result.

For me a great example in learning to see others in a more compassionate way was in politics. I am a very liberal political person and when I was younger and in college I was very active in politics but then I started on a spiritual path and I realized that the feelings of anger and even hatred I felt to the people on the other side of my political views was a real barrier to opening myself up.

There was a period when I was a student in Ann Arbor where I really hated Richard Nixon. Me and my friends would watch the news and just spew hatred at him. I really felt like I wanted him to die. But then as I started on the path of awakening to my spiritual side I became aware that this was really not a tenable position. You cannot see the divine nature in all human beings and then wish them ill to the point of wishing that they would drop dead. To cultivate compassion I had to scale back on my political leanings and my political activity because I just found it too difficult to practice compassion and be that active in politics.

That is an example of where I changed my behavior to allow the compassion to come out more. Now, as I write this book, there is a lot of conflict between liberals and conservatives. And as I see all these people rallying against the things I believe in and even saying hateful things, I have an opportunity to practice compassion toward those people and to see that they are in fact suffering.

I can see that they are coming out of a place of fear and that their fear makes them suffer way more than the irritation that I feel by observing their actions and the things that they are saying. And I would say I am doing better than before but at times they still bug the hell out of me, which gives me an opportunity to practice what I preach.

The bottom line is that you do not have to like everyone but you need to try to love everyone in the sense of that compassionate, universal divine love we have been discussing. That is the practice that everybody can do and you will find that it can be a good start to lead you down the spiritual path.

The Importance of Meditation

Meditation may seem intimidating but it really is not; it is something that anybody can do. You can do it without being involved in any kind of teaching or having to commit to any group although, as I mentioned before, groups can make your work easier.

Meditating is really the way that you can take control of your development of your self-awareness. And the importance of it, as we talked about before, is that when you meditate the basic thing that you are doing is quieting your thinking mind. You are quieting that thinking–ego mind of thoughts and words and when you quiet that ego mind, the divine mind is always there, it is always shining.

Immediately when you quiet your thinking mind, the divine mind has more energy and a presence in your consciousness, in your aware consciousness. Now of course there is a learning curve here. When you first start meditating you may not immediately notice a change because you will be surprised at how much your mind is filled with thoughts and words and energy. However, as you stick with it you will soon be able to quiet all that mind chatter. That is why it is called a meditation practice, because you do have to keep practicing. As you do it more and more you train your mind to quiet those thoughts. And the very first thing that is involved in any real meditation practice is your breathing.

Breathing is a major part of a meditative practice because controlling our breathing is the only control we have over an involuntary body system. We breathe without thinking about it. We breathe whether or not we are aware of it just as our heart pumps whether or not we are aware of it.

Our kidneys continue to work whether or not we are aware of it. Our heart beats day and night without us giving it a thought. Our brain is firing off whether or not we are aware of it. All of these systems are working whether or not we are aware of them, but our breathing is the one involuntary system that we can easily control.

The pace at which we are breathing, how slowly we breathe, the amount of air we are bringing in, all of that is something that we can control. And as we control our breathing, we automatically start to signal our brain to calm down.

The more that you learn how to control your breathing, the more you will slow down your thoughts and this is the first step in being able to gain control over your thinking mind. You can see this clearly when you get stressed out or upset. Your brain is racing and if you just stop and take a deep breath and let it out slowly, you immediately see that your thoughts slow down a bit. Short quick breathing will increase anxiety and long slow breathing will calm you down.

That is the first thing we tell someone who is excited, or upset, "take a deep breath." Why is that? Well, because of what we just said. Taking the deep breath is allowing the mind to immediately calm down. If we can do that in a regular practice then we begin to train the mind to calm down and when we go into a meditative practice, when we start to do that breathing, we get more and more into that state of awareness, a state of quietude of the mind that allows the divine mind to shine through.

The very first thing that you can do is just sit and control your breath and watch your mind, watch your thoughts. This is basic Zen practice which is to sit with your spine straight, breathe slowly and just watch your thoughts as they appear in your mind.

It is important to sit with your spine as straight as possible without strain because you want to allow the neural energy to flow freely up and down your spine. The practice is to just sit quietly and watch your thoughts as if you are watching clouds drift by. Over time the goal is that you just let all your thoughts drift away and eventually your mind will be still.

Now, personally I found that to be a very difficult practice and for me I got much more out of what are referred to as guided meditations. In a guided meditation you focus on a symbol or words or sounds. The idea here is that you focus your mind on something and that over time this will also empty your mind of other thoughts and leave it quiet and still.

These types of guided meditation take different forms. One type can be to focus on a set of phrases, which could be considered like a prayer. Or you can use a mantra which usually is a sound, certain syllables, or small group of words repeated in a more rhythmic way. You may also focus on a symbol or picture that has spiritual significance along with repeating some sort of prayer or mantra.

The more you repeat this type of practice the more it will quiet your mind. If you keep practicing then these meditations will help get you deeper into a state of awareness and if you keep at it they can lead you to transcendental states; to states of awareness where you make a complete connection with the Divine mind.

But controlling your breathing is the first step and then you can move on to the more advanced meditative practices. If you do not have a practice and want to begin to meditate you can find more information on how to meditate on my website: www.GodForGrownUps.com. I have a meditation program for sale that you can download which teaches basic and advanced meditation techniques.

Big Questions - Final Thoughts

At the beginning of this book I wrote that we would answer some very fundamental, yet profound, questions. Does God exist? If so what is the nature of God? What is my true spiritual nature, my connection to God? And the big one – Why am I here?

Does God exist? We have established that, for most people, our intuition, our beliefs and even our science point to the idea that we live in a creation as opposed to a random series of events. If there is a creation there must be a creator. And it seems unlikely that the Creator of All That Is would not still be a part of that creation.

If God does exist what is the nature of God? A more mature understanding of God is the understanding that God is not a being as we understand that term. We live in a finite world but God is part of the infinite – beyond our time-space reality and in one sense we can never totally understand that nature. But we have seen that consciousness may also go beyond time and space and that gives us our taste of the infinite. We have also seen that God is never angry and does not make rules or punish us. God is in fact pure eternal love and compassion.

What is my true spiritual nature, my connection to God? It is important to remember that God is everywhere, is in all of us and that we are in fact a manifestation of God come forward to play in this reality. We are Eternal Divine beings having a human experience in this time-space reality. All of creation is vibrational and the highest vibrations are consciousness.

When we understand that all of us are a manifestation of God, and that this manifestation is consciousness, then we can see that each of us is a divine being. This recognition opens us up to many more possible connections to other human beings and opens us up to the idea that *We Are All One*, that we all share the same divine spark and therefore we are literally brothers and sisters to everyone in the world.

We have seen that we are blocked from our divine nature by our thinking-ego mind that is caught up in our day to day lives. And while this thinking-ego mind is totally necessary to have a normal human life, it is also the barrier to our divine mind. By understanding this, and with practice, we can clear the obstructions of the thinking-ego mind and allow the divine mind to shine through.

Why are we here? To be human beings! To create a human life and human love and through that to allow God to experience the creation through us, our purpose is that simple and that profound.

I thank you for allowing me to share my thoughts with you. I hope that this has helped your understanding of the nature of God and the nature of our Divine Self which are one and the same. And I hope that this new understanding benefits you on your spiritual path – whatever that may be. I wish you the best of life and the most wondrous, joyous journey towards love, light and happiness.

ABOUT THE AUTHOR

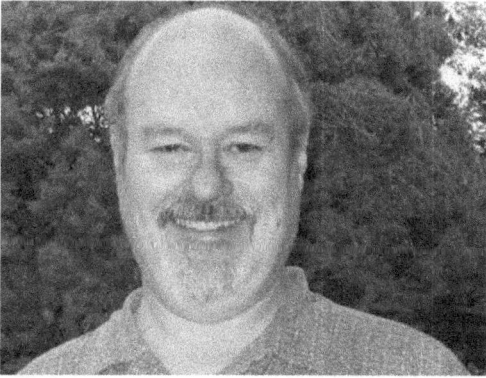

Bob Garrity was born in New Jersey and spent his formative teen and early adult years in Saginaw, Michigan and then at the University of Michigan in Ann Arbor. He moved to California in 1976 and since 1999 has lived in Mill Valley, CA with his wife April.

Bob has been on the spiritual path for almost 40 years and had a life changing experience at the age of 19 which has led, over time, to a deep understanding of our place in the Divine scheme. He is initiated into the Chisti Sufi Order and took refuge in the Kagyu Buddhist tradition and has spent over 25 years as a student in the Arica School, a modern mystical school. He also served on the Board of Directors of The Arica Institute and founded and currently serves on the Board of Directors of Awakening the Diamond Mind Foundation.

In addition to his spiritual pursuits he had a successful business career including key management positions at Viacom Cable and Excite@Home. He received a Bachelor of Science degree from the University of San Francisco in Information Technology.

Recently he has been concentrating on internet projects and runs a number of web sites. He has started a social network for spiritual seekers – www.AwareVillage.com and has more information on spiritual topics along with his meditation training program at –
www.GodForGrownUps.com

Suggested Reading:

Buddhism
The Way of Zen – Alan Watts
An Introduction to Zen Buddhism – D.T. Suzuki
The Three Pillars of Zen – Roshi Philip Kapleau
The Art of Happiness – Dali Lama
Tantirc Mysticism of Tibet – John Bloefeld
Tibetan Book of Living and Dying – Sogyal Rinpoche

Sufism
The Way of the Sufi – Idres Shah
Learning How to Learn – Idres Shah
Mastery Through Accomplishment – Hazrat Inyat Khan

Christianity
The Gnostic Gospels – Elaine Pagels
Christian Mystics – Mathew Fox

Law of Attraction
Life Lessons for Mastering the Law of Attraction – Eva Gregory, Jeanna Gabellini, Jack Canfield, Mark Victor Hansen

Physics
The Self Aware Universe – Amit Goswami
The Tao of Physics – Fritjof Capra

Other
Interviews with Oscar Ichazo – Oscar Ichazo
Facets of Unity – A.H. Almaas
Plotinus or The Simplicity of Vision – Pierre Hadot
Autobiography of a Yogi – Paramahansa Yogananda
In Search of the Miraculous – P.D. Ouspensky
Toward a Psychology of Being – Abraham Maslow

Stay in Touch:

You can follow me on twitter:

@BobGarrity

Or on Facebook:

www.facebook.com/pages/God-for-Grownups/

To purchase my meditation program go to:

www.GodForGrownUps.com/meditation

For more information on spiritual topics and to connect with other spiritual seekers visit:

www.AwareVillage.com